Isaac Asimov's 21st Century Library of the Universe

The Solar System

Uranus

BY ISAAC ASIMOV
WITH REVISIONS AND UPDATING BY RICHARD HANTULA

Gareth Stevens Publishing
A WORLD ALMANAC EDUCATION GROUP COMPANY

Please visit our web site at: **www.garethstevens.com**
For a free color catalog describing Gareth Stevens Publishing's list of high-quality
books and multimedia programs, call 1-800-542-2595 (USA) or 1-800-387-3178 (Canada).
Gareth Stevens Publishing's fax: (414) 332-3567.

Library of Congress Cataloging-in-Publication Data

Asimov, Isaac.
    Uranus / by Isaac Asimov; with revisions and updating by Richard Hantula.
       p. cm. – (Isaac Asimov's 21st century library of the universe. The solar system)
    Rev. ed. of: A distant puzzle: the planet Uranus. 1994.
    Summary: Introduces the third largest known planet in the solar system.
    Includes bibliographical references and index.
    ISBN 0-8368-3243-4 (lib. bdg.)
    1. Uranus (Planet)–Juvenile literature. [1. Uranus (Planet).] I. Hantula, Richard.
II. Asimov, Isaac. Distant puzzle: the planet Uranus. III. Title. IV. Isaac Asimov's 21st
century library of the universe. Solar system.
    QB681.A85   2002
    523.47–dc21   2002021682

This edition first published in 2002 by
Gareth Stevens Publishing
A World Almanac Education Group Company
330 West Olive Street, Suite 100
Milwaukee, WI 53212 USA

Series editor: Betsy Rasmussen
Cover design and layout adaptation: Melissa Valuch
Picture research: Kathy Keller
Additional picture research: Diane Laska-Swanke
Artwork commissioning: Kathy Keller and Laurie Shock
Production director: Susan Ashley

The editors at Gareth Stevens Publishing have selected science author Richard Hantula to bring
this classic series of young people's information books up to date. Richard Hantula has written
and edited books and articles on science and technology for more than two decades. He was
the senior U.S. editor for the *Macmillan Encyclopedia of Science*.

In addition to Hantula's contribution to this most recent edition, the editors would like to
acknowledge the participation of two noted science authors, Greg Walz-Chojnacki and
Francis Reddy, as contributors to earlier editions of this work.

Printed in the United States of America

1 2 3 4 5 6 7 8 9 06 05 04 03 02

Contents

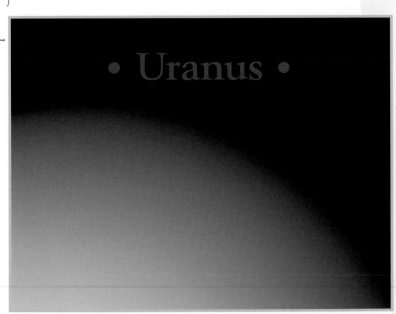

• Uranus •

We live in an enormously large place — the Universe. It is only natural that we would want to understand this place, so scientists and engineers have developed instruments and spacecrafts that have told us far more about the Universe than we could possibly imagine.

We have seen planets up close, and spacecrafts have even landed on some. We have learned about quasars and pulsars, supernovas and colliding galaxies, and black holes and dark matter. We have gathered amazing data about how the Universe may have come into being and how it may end. Nothing could be more astonishing.

We have learned a great deal about an unusual giant planet in our Solar System that is tipped over on its side. This planet, Uranus, was named for the ancient Greek god of the heavens. Even when it is closest to Earth, Uranus is still more than $1\frac{1}{2}$ billion miles ($2\frac{1}{2}$ billion kilometers) away. Before 1986, we could see it only as a tiny spot of light through our telescopes. Now we have seen it up close and know much more about it and about the moons that circle it.

In 1986, the space probe *Voyager 2* took this picture of Uranus from a distance of about 600,000 miles (1,000,000 kilometers). *Voyager* found that the planet has more rings and moons than had been thought.

A Modern-Day Planet

In 1781, in England, a German-born astronomer named William Herschel studied the sky with a telescope he built himself. On March 13, he saw a little spot of light where no such spot should be. He thought it might be a comet, but it was not fuzzy looking as comets usually are. It moved slowly, night by night.

Herschel soon realized that it circled the Sun far beyond Saturn, the most distant planet then known. It was a new, still more distant planet. All the other planets had been known since ancient times. This new planet — the first one to be discovered in modern times — was eventually given the name Uranus.

Herschel (*left*) discovered two of Uranus's moons with this huge telescope (*right*), which he built after he found the planet.

The quiet giant

Uranus is much farther away than the planets known from ancient times, and so it is much dimmer. It also moves more slowly. In 1690, an English astronomer, John Flamsteed, saw what he thought was a dim star in the constellation Taurus.

He called it 34 Tauri and marked it on his map. It was actually Uranus. If Flamsteed had gone back to look at it a few nights later, he would have noticed that it had moved. So Uranus was actually seen 91 years before it was identified.

Discovery in Motion

What have we learned about this modern planet? Well, even without the help of the *Voyager 2* space probe, astronomers could determine some facts about Uranus by watching its motion.

It is, on average, about 1,780,000,000 miles (2,870,000,000 km) from the Sun. That is 19 times as far from the Sun as Earth is. Uranus's size can be determined by measuring how wide the planet looks at that distance. Its diameter is 31,763 miles (51,118 km), which is four times the diameter of Earth. Uranus has a mass nearly 15 times that of Earth, making it a giant planet. It is much smaller than Jupiter, though. Jupiter, the largest planet, is over 20 times as massive as Uranus. Uranus is also much smaller than Saturn. The fourth giant planet, Neptune, is slightly smaller than Uranus, but it has more mass.

Bode's Law: too good to be true!

In 1766, the German mathematician Johann Daniel Titius found a simple formula that showed how far each planet ought to be from the Sun. German astronomer Johann Bode thought the formula was important, and in 1772, he called it to everyone's attention. It was named "Bode's Law" for that reason. When Uranus was discovered in 1781, it turned out to be at about the distance from the Sun predicted by Bode's Law. When Neptune was discovered, however, it did not fit Bode's Law. For that reason, astronomers stopped using the law.

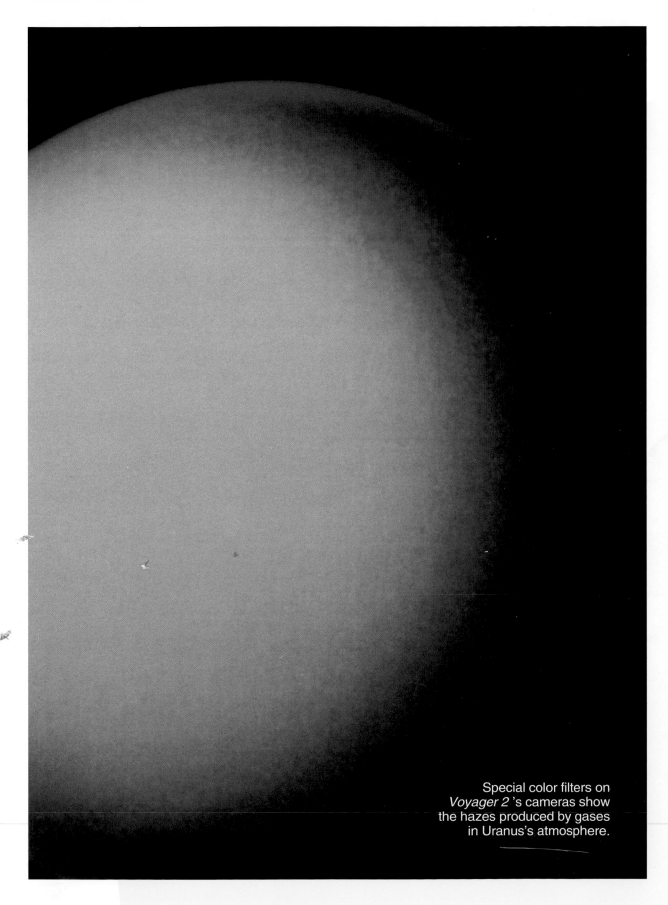

Special color filters on
Voyager 2 's cameras show
the hazes produced by gases
in Uranus's atmosphere.

The Sideways Planet

Uranus is so far away that for about 200 years, scientists could not determine how quickly it turns on its axis. They could tell there was something odd about the turning, though. Most planets turn on their axis in such a way that they are almost upright as they move around the Sun. Earth's axis is tipped only 1/4 of the way from the vertical.

Uranus's axis, however, is tipped so far that the planet seems to be rolling on its side as it moves around the Sun. Some people like to call Uranus the "sideways planet." The only other planet in the Solar System with a sideways axis is remote Pluto, which is so small some astronomers think it should not even count as a planet.

Above: Small, solid bodies, called planetesimals, may have existed at an early time in our Solar System. Some scientists think that collisions between planetesimals and a newly formed planet could alter the planet's tilt. Here, an artist imagines two planetesimals colliding and fragmenting into smaller planetesimals.

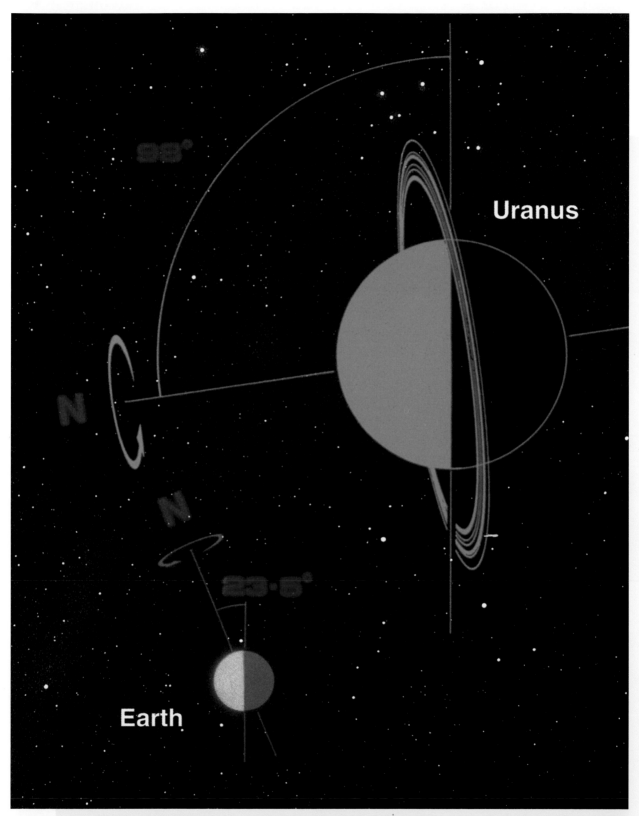

Above: Uranus is known as the sideways planet, because the axis on which it rotates is tilted roughly 90° from the vertical. Earth, as you can see, is only slightly tilted in its rotation.

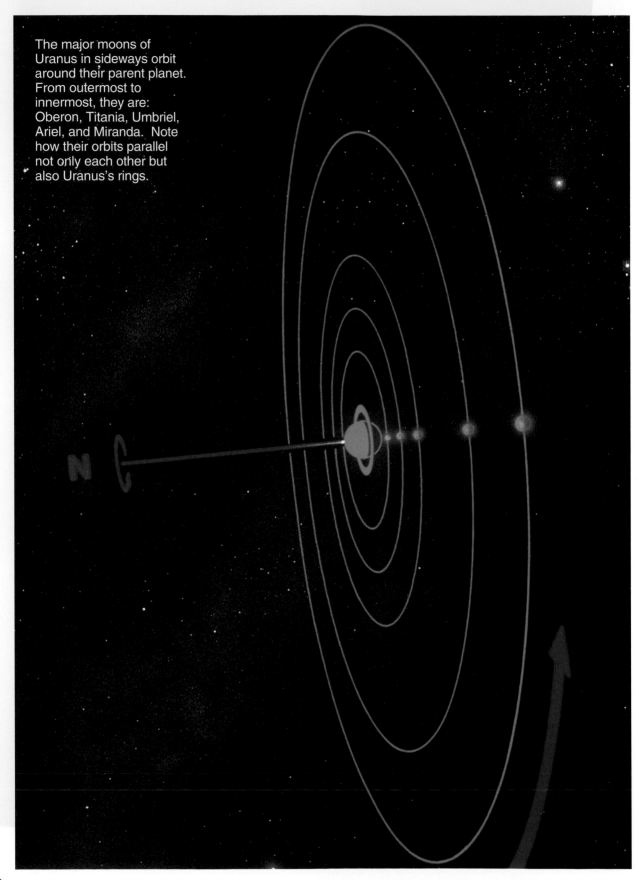

The major moons of Uranus in sideways orbit around their parent planet. From outermost to innermost, they are: Oberon, Titania, Umbriel, Ariel, and Miranda. Note how their orbits parallel not only each other but also Uranus's rings.

Literary Moons

Like most planets, Uranus has moons, or satellites. These smaller worlds travel in orbits around Uranus – just as our Moon circles Earth. Two were discovered by Herschel in 1787. He named them Oberon and Titania, after the king and queen of fairies in one of William Shakespeare's plays. Two more moons were discovered 64 years later. One was named Ariel, after a fairy in another of Shakespeare's plays, and the second was called Umbriel, after a character in a poem by Alexander Pope.

In 1948, a fifth satellite was discovered orbiting Uranus and was named Miranda, in honor of another of Shakespeare's characters. All these moons' orbits are tipped just as the planet's axis is. From Earth, the moons seem to go up and down, not side to side, like other planets' moons.

Left: A "family portrait" of the largest Uranian moons (*top to bottom*): Miranda, Ariel, Umbriel, Titania, and Oberon. They are all named after characters in English literature. This composite photo shows how big these satellites are in relation to one another. Titania and Oberon, the two largest, are nearly the same size. Titania is 980 miles (1,580 km) in diameter, and Oberon is 945 miles (1,520 km) in diameter.

Introducing the planet Herschel?

When Uranus was discovered, Herschel wanted to call it Georgium Sidus (Latin for "George's Star") in honor of the British king George III. Some astronomers suggested calling it Herschel in honor of its discoverer. Here is how the planet was finally named. Beyond Earth, there is Mars. Then there is Jupiter, who is Mars's father in mythology; next comes Saturn, who is Jupiter's father. So the new planet was called Uranus, after Saturn's father.

Another World with Rings

In 1977, Uranus moved in front of a star. Astronomers watched closely, because they wanted to measure how the starlight dimmed as Uranus's atmosphere passed in front of it. That would tell them something about the atmosphere. To their surprise, the star "blinked out" several times *before* the atmosphere moved in front of it. It "blinked out" again several more times after Uranus and its atmosphere had moved away. From this, scientists determined that Uranus has rings circling it, just like Saturn. Saturn's rings are huge and bright, but Uranus's rings are very thin and dark.

Left: The dark ring system of Uranus shows up best when lit from behind, but such a view is impossible from Earth. The *Voyager 2* spacecraft took this picture of the rings when it raced past Uranus in 1986. The ring system consists of ten narrow rings of rock or ice particles, a broad ring of dust, and dozens of dusty ringlets.

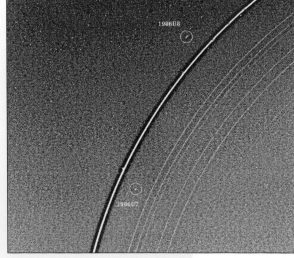

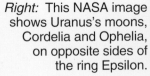

Right: This NASA image shows Uranus's moons, Cordelia and Ophelia, on opposite sides of the ring Epsilon.

Like Saturn's rings, the rings of Uranus are not solid. Instead, they are made of millions of chunks of rock and ice as well as smaller particles and dust.

This photo of Uranus was taken by
Voyager 2 from 153 million miles
(247 million km) away, on July 15,
1985 — six months before the craft's
January 1986 flyby. This was the
first real chance for scientists to see
the relation of the planet to its
moons. In this composite picture,
several of the moons can be seen.

A Challenging Planet

Astronomers were excited by the surprising discovery of rings around Uranus in the 1970s, but it did not seem as though they would ever find out more information about the planet. It was so far away that it just looked like a little blue-green circle of light. Jupiter and Saturn, two planets that are closer to Earth and larger than Uranus, can be seen much more easily. In fact, these two giants appear so clearly in telescopes that markings on the surfaces can be seen. The markings move over the surfaces, and we can see how fast these planets rotate. Uranus, small and dim, did not show markings, however. This puzzled scientists for over 200 years.

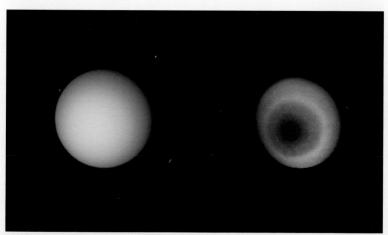

Above: Two views of Uranus. The left picture shows how the planet would appear to a person in a spacecraft 11 million miles (18 million km) from Uranus. The right picture is taken through color filters and enhanced by computer to show the gases present on and around Uranus. In both shots, the view is toward the planet's pole of rotation, which lies just left of center.

An artist's conception of *Voyager 2*'s flyby of Uranus. The probe came closest to Uranus on January 24, 1986.

Above: Landing on a gaseous planet like Uranus would be impossible since the planet really has no land. As this cutaway picture shows, many scientists think the planet consists of three layers — a core of rock and ice, surrounded by a layer of liquid and an outer layer of gas.

Probing the Planet

Today, we have learned far more about Uranus than we knew even as recently as the early 1980s. We have built space probes, and they have traveled to the distant planets. *Voyager 1* and *Voyager 2* were sent into space in 1977. Both *Voyager* probes passed Jupiter and Saturn, taking photographs as they flew by. *Voyager 2* had its course arranged so that it continued toward Uranus. It passed Uranus in January 1986 and photographed it. This was not easy, because Uranus is so far from the Sun that it gets only $1/360$ as much light as we do. *Voyager 2* had to take pictures in this dim light as it was moving past, but it did a magnificent job.

Now that *Voyager 2* has flown past Uranus, scientists know much more about this giant planet, although many questions remain. Some astronomers think that Uranus has a small core of rock and ice. This core, which might be as large as Earth, may be surrounded by a thick "sea" containing water and rock. On top of that is the atmosphere, which some scientists believe may be as deep as 7,000 miles (11,000 km) or more. It contains mainly hydrogen and helium, plus smaller amounts of methane and other gases. With so much of the planet made up of a gaseous atmosphere, Uranus is one of the gas giants — joining the group that includes Jupiter, Saturn, and Neptune.

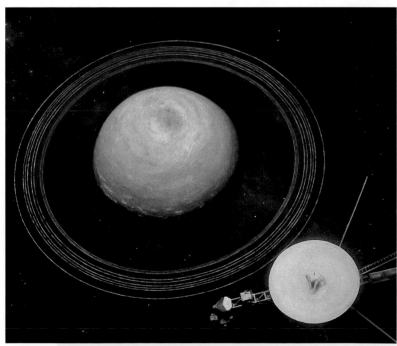

Above: An artist imagines *Voyager 2* taking images of Uranus before heading to Neptune for a look.

Important Clues

Voyager 2's photographs were beamed back to Earth. They showed Uranus much more clearly than we could see it with a telescope from Earth. It still looked like just a bluish globe, however. In a way, this was not very surprising. Sunlight powers the winds on Earth and also provides some of the energy fueling the complex motion that occurs in the atmospheres of Jupiter and Saturn. Since Uranus receives much less sunlight, it seemed natural that it would have a much quieter atmosphere.

Still, *Voyager* found that Uranus has bright, thin clouds deep in the planet's atmosphere. Meanwhile, radio signals showed that it takes Uranus about $17\frac{1}{4}$ hours to turn on its axis. Until then, guesses had been anywhere from 10 to 25 hours.

Scientists were delighted that they could now compare the motions of the clouds to Uranus's spin, because that information gives them important clues about the way weather works on Uranus.

A cloud on Uranus. This *Voyager 2* photograph shows a cloud along the bluish edge of the planet. This photo was taken through color filters and enhanced by computer. In true color, the cloud would have been nearly invisible.

19

Moons and More Moons

Uranus has more than two dozen moons. Only five are large enough to be seen with ordinary telescopes from Earth. Ten of the planet's moons were found by *Voyager 2* in 1986, and several more were discovered by astronomers later. The smallest ones are only about 6 miles (10 km) wide. Like much of the material in the rings, the small moons are dark as coal.

Of the five big moons, Umbriel is the darkest. A bright circle stands out on its battered gray surface like a powdered doughnut on a dark plate. Perhaps the circle is bright, clean ice dug up by a recent collision. A strange, dark material coats the floor of one of the craters on Oberon, the big moon farthest from Uranus. On the largest moon, Titania, a giant valley stretching over 1,000 miles (1,600 km) shows where the moon's frozen crust split open long ago.

Left: A *Voyager 2* picture of Oberon that shows several large impact craters.

Why are Uranus's rings so dark?

If the rings were composed only of icy particles, they would reflect most of the light that falls on them and would glitter brightly. Instead, they appear dark. Perhaps the rings began as a mixture of ice and rock, and the ice slowly evaporated, leaving the rock behind. Saturn's bright rings have not evaporated, though, and Saturn gets four times as much sunlight as Uranus. Perhaps the real mystery is why Saturn's rings are so bright.

Above: Titania has fewer large craters than Oberon. Flows of ice and rock probably flooded Titania's oldest and largest craters when the moon was still young. Its surface expanded and cracked as it cooled, creating giant valleys hundreds of miles long.

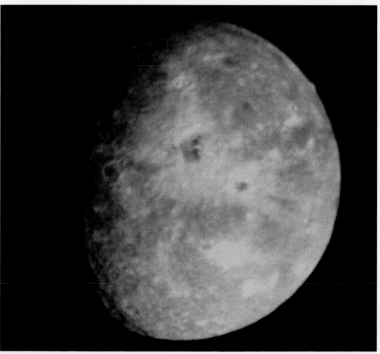

Left: A dark mix of ice and rock oozed out of Oberon's interior to fill the crater near the center of this picture.

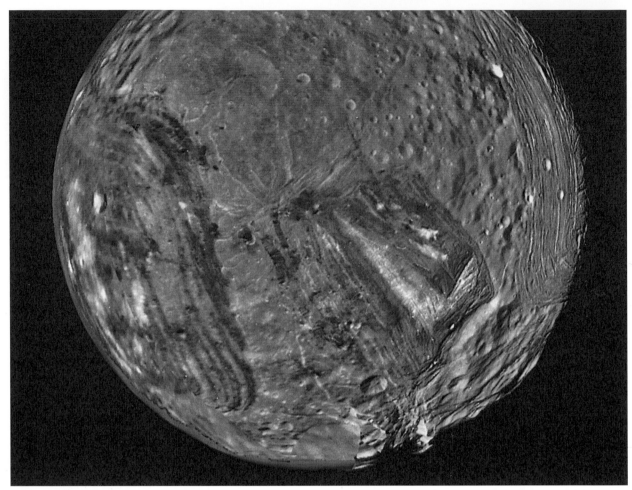

Above: Nine *Voyager 2* images were combined and processed by computer to create this portrait of Miranda. The bright cliffs of a valley much deeper than Earth's Grand Canyon are visible at the bottom. The moon's south pole is at the center.

Right: Miranda's terrain has grooves that could reach depths of a mile or more. One day, probes, like the lander imagined by the artist here, may discover important information about Uranus and its moons.

Cracked Worlds

Large craters pepper the faces of Umbriel, Oberon, and Titania. Ariel has an interesting network of crisscrossing valleys. Scientists believe the valleys formed when Ariel's surface cooled, expanded, and cracked. Icy material — possibly frozen water and ammonia — then oozed out of the moon's cracks. It coated the valley floors, smoothed the surface, and buried many craters.

Miranda, a moon just 290 miles (470 km) in diameter, rates as one of the strangest worlds in the Solar System. Pictures of it show cratered plains, a deep valley, and unusual areas etched by curving grooves and ridges. Some scientists think that as this moon formed, rocky material began to sink toward its center, and icy material (the grooved regions) started to rise toward the surface. Tiny Miranda froze solid before this process was finished, however, leaving the jumbled world that *Voyager 2* photographed.

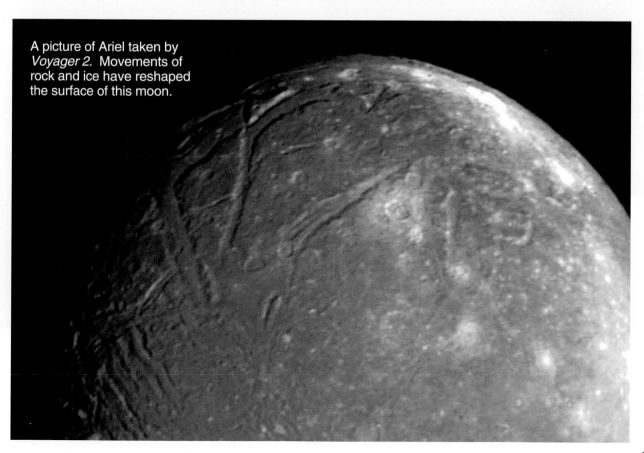

A picture of Ariel taken by *Voyager 2*. Movements of rock and ice have reshaped the surface of this moon.

More
Interesting
Than We Think

In the pictures of Uranus made by *Voyager 2* in
1986, the planet seemed to show very little detail.
Some people called it the most boring planet in the
Solar System. Scientists expected Neptune would
turn out to look much the same as Uranus, a colored
gas ball with few clouds or storms to be seen. Yet,
when *Voyager 2* flew past Neptune in 1989, it
found a violent atmosphere. A storm the size of our
entire Earth, dubbed the Great Dark Spot, was visible on
Neptune long before the spacecraft reached the planet.
Closer in, the probe photographed wispy white clouds
racing around the planet, driven by some of the fastest
winds in the Solar System.

So why wasn't Uranus like Neptune? Well, perhaps
it is, at least a little. In the years after *Voyager 2*
left Uranus, astronomers, using the Hubble Space
Telescope and Earth-based telescopes, observed
a dark spot and other intriguing patterns in
the planet's atmosphere. Perhaps the
weather on Uranus is more interesting
than we think and *Voyager 2*
caught it during an
inactive period.

Above: A 1998 Hubble Space Telescope image of Uranus showing clouds.

A Century Beyond

The pictures and data sent back by *Voyager 2* made it possible for astronomers to study Uranus, its rings, and its satellites in detail. The information provided by the probe, however, could not answer all the questions scientists have about Uranus. A return visit to the planet will be needed to deal with some of these questions. It may be many years before another probe is launched to study Uranus. In the meantime, scientists have gotten much useful information and valuable pictures from instruments in orbit around Earth, such as the Hubble Space Telescope, and also from advanced instruments located on Earth's surface.

Still, scientists want to make a return visit to Uranus. By the time a new mission is launched, we will probably have more advanced probes that can study the planet in greater detail. Who knows? Perhaps the next probe will even carry humans with it.

Could this child be a
future relative of yours?
He or she could be
one of the first to travel
to Uranus.

The Moons of Uranus

Tiny moons discovered after 1999 not shown.

Name	Diameter	Distance from Uranus
Cordelia	15 miles (25 km)	30,925 miles (49,770 km)
Ophelia	18 miles (30 km)	33,420 miles (53,790 km)
Bianca	25 miles (40 km)	36,765 miles (59,170 km)
Cressida	37 miles (60 km)	38,390 miles (61,780 km)
Desdemona	35 miles (55 km)	38,950 miles (62,680 km)
Juliet	50 miles (85 km)	39,985 miles (64,350 km)
Portia	65 miles (110 km)	41,065 miles (66,090 km)
Rosalind	35 miles (55 km)	43,460 miles (69,940 km)
Belinda	40 miles (65 km)	46,760 miles (75,260 km)
Puck	95 miles (155 km)	53,440 miles (86,010 km)
Miranda	290 miles (470 km)	80,400 miles (129,390 km)
Ariel	720 miles (1,160 km)	118,690 miles (191,020 km)
Umbriel	725 miles (1,170 km)	165,470 miles (266,300 km)
Titania	980 miles (1,580 km)	270,860 miles (435,910 km)
Oberon	945 miles (1,520 km)	362,580 miles (583,520 km)
Caliban	37 miles (60 km)	4,450,000 miles (7,169,000 km)
Stephano	12 miles (20 km)	4,900,000 miles (7,900,000 km)
Sycorax	75 miles (120 km)	7,590,000 miles (12,214,000 km)
Prospero	12 miles (20 km)	10,000,000 miles (16,100,000 km)
Setebos	12 miles (20 km)	13,450,000 miles (21,650,000 km)

Fact File: Day and Night

Uranus is the third-largest known planet in the Solar System, and the seventh-farthest planet from the Sun. It is also one of the most unusual planets. Its axis is tipped on its side. As a result, each pole faces the Sun during half of Uranus's 84-year orbit. This means that each half of Uranus has a 42-year-long "day" of sunlight followed by a 42-year-long "night" of darkness.

The Sun and its family of planets
(*left to right*): Mercury, Venus, Earth,
Mars, Jupiter, Saturn, Uranus,
Neptune, Pluto.

Uranus

Right: A close-up of
Uranus and its five
major satellites
(*top to bottom*):
Miranda, Ariel, Umbriel,
Titania, and Oberon.

Uranus:
How It Measures Up to Earth

Planet	Diameter	Rotation Period (length of day)	Period of Orbit around Sun (length of year)	Known Moons	Surface Gravity	Distance from Sun (nearest-farthest)	Least Time for Light to Travel to Earth
Uranus	31,763 miles (51,118 km)	17 hours, 14 minutes	30,685 days (84.01 years)	24+	0.89*	1.70–1.87 billion miles (2.74–3.00 billion km)	2.4 hours
Earth	7,926 miles (12,756 km)	23 hours, 56 minutes	365.256 days (1 year)	1	1.00*	91.3–94.4 million miles (147–152 million km)	–

* Multiply your weight by this number to find out how much you would weigh on this planet. In the case of Uranus, which lacks a surface, the number is for cloud-top level.

More Books about Uranus

DK Space Encyclopedia. Nigel Henbest and Heather Couper (DK Publishing)

Jupiter, Saturn, Uranus, and Neptune. Gregory Vogt (Raintree Steck-Vaughn)

Uranus. Larry Dane Brimner (Children's Press)

Uranus. Seymour Simon (Mulberry Books)

CD-ROMs and DVDs

CD-ROM: *Exploring the Planets.* (Cinegram)

DVD: *The Voyager Odyssey.* (Image Entertainment)

Web Sites

The Internet is a good place to get more information about Uranus. The web sites listed here can help you learn about the most recent discoveries, as well as those made in the past.

Nine Planets. www.nineplanets.org/uranus.html

StarDate Online. stardate.org/resources/ssguide/uranus.html

Views of the Solar System. www.solarviews.com/eng/uranus.htm

Voyager Project. voyager.jpl.nasa.gov/

Windows to the Universe. www.windows.ucar.edu/tour/link=/uranus/uranus.html

Places to Visit

Here are some museums and centers where you can find a variety of space exhibits.

American Museum of Natural History
Central Park West at 79th Street
New York, NY 10024

Canada Science and Technology Museum
1867 St. Laurent Boulevard
Science Park
100 Queen's Park
Ottawa, Ontario K1G 5A3
Canada

Henry Crown Space Center
Museum of Science and Industry
57th Street and Lake Shore Drive
Chicago, IL 60637

Lawrence Hall of Science
Centennial Drive
Berkely, CA 94720

National Air and Space Museum
Smithsonian Institution
7th and Independence Avenue SW
Washington, DC 20560

Odyssium
11211 142nd Street
Edmonton, Alberta T5M 4A1
Canada

Scienceworks Museum
2 Booker Street
Spotswood
Melbourne, Victoria 3015
Australia

Virginia Air and Space Center
600 Settlers Landing Road
Hampton, VA 23669

Glossary

astronomer: a scientist who studies the worlds beyond our Earth, including the other planets, the stars, comets, and more.

atmosphere: the gases that surround a planet, star, or moon. The atmosphere of Uranus contains hydrogen, helium, and other gases.

axis: an imaginary line through the center of an object such as a planet, star, or moon around which the object rotates. The axis of Uranus is tilted so that the planet appears to be on its side compared to most other planets in our Solar System.

Bode's Law: a formula that was believed to show how far each planet should be from our Sun. Johann Daniel Titius developed the formula in 1766. It later turned out to be false.

crater: a hole in the ground caused by a volcanic explosion or the impact of an object.

diameter: a straight line across the center of a circle or sphere from one side to the other.

gravity: the force that causes objects like planets and their moons to be attracted to one another.

helium: a light, colorless gas that, along with hydrogen and a few other gases, makes up the atmosphere of Uranus.

Herschel, William: a German-born astronomer working in England who discovered Uranus in 1781.

Hubble Space Telescope: an artificial satellite containing a telescope and related instruments that was placed in orbit around Earth in 1990.

mass: the quantity or amount of matter in an object.

moon: a small body in space that moves in an orbit around a larger body. A moon is said to be a satellite of the larger body.

orbit: the path that one celestial object follows as it circles, or revolves, around another.

planet: one of the large bodies that revolve around a star like our Sun. Our Earth and Uranus are planets in our Solar System.

planetesimals: small chunks of matter that, when joined together, may have formed planets.

probe: a craft that travels in space, photographing and studying celestial bodies and in some cases even landing on them.

rings: bits of matter that circle some planets, including Uranus.

Solar System: the Sun with the planets and all the other bodies, such as the asteroids, that orbit the Sun.

Sun: our star and the provider of the energy that makes life possible on Earth.

Uranus: ancient Greek god of the heavens and the father of Saturn. The planet Uranus is named for him.

***Voyager 2*:** the space probe that sent back to Earth valuable information about Uranus in 1986.

Index

Born in 1920, Isaac Asimov came to the United States as a young boy from his native Russia. As a young man, he was a student of biochemistry. In time, he became one of the most productive writers the world has ever known. His books cover a spectrum of topics, including science, history, language theory, fantasy, and science fiction. His brilliant imagination gained him the respect and admiration of adults and children alike. Sadly, Isaac Asimov died shortly after the publication of the first edition of *Isaac Asimov's Library of the Universe*.

The publishers wish to thank the following for permission to reproduce copyright material: front cover, 3, NASA/JPL; 4, NASA; 5 (left), National Maritime Museum; 5 (right), Royal Astronomical Society; 6, NASA/JPL; 7, NASA; 8, © David Hardy; 9, 10, © Julian Baum 1988; 11, NASA; 12 (left), NASA/JPL; 12 (right), National Space Science Data Center and the Team Leader, Dr. Bradford A. Smith; 13, © David Hardy; 14, NASA; 15, NASA/JPL; 16 (large), © Julian Baum 1986; 16 (inset), © Lynette Cook 1988; 17, © Julian Baum 1986; 18-19, United States Geological Survey; 20, 21 (lower), NASA/JPL; 21 (upper), © MariLynn Flynn 1982; 22 (upper), Frank Reddy; 22 (lower), © Alan Gutierrez 1979; 23, National Space Science Data Center and the Team Leader, Dr. Bradford A. Smith; 24-25, NASA/JPL; 25, Erich Karkoschka, University of Arizona, and NASA; 26-27, Courtesy of Spaceweek National Headquarters; 28-29 (all), © Sally Bensusen 1987.